By God's Design

NINDYL TRAVERS

By God's Design by Nindyl Travers
Copyright © 2018 by Nindyl Travers

All rights reserved. This book is protected under the copyright laws of the United States of America. This book may not be copied or reprinted for commercial gain or profit. The use of short quotations or occasional page copying for personal or group study is permitted and encouraged.

All Scripture quotations, unless otherwise indicated, are taken from the King James Version (KJV), Public Domain

Scripture quotations marked (AMP) are taken from Amplified Bible, Copyright © 2015 by The Lockman Foundation, La Habra, CA 90631. All rights reserved.

Scripture quotations marked (AMPC) are taken from Amplified Bible, Classic Edition, Copyright © 1954, 1958, 1962, 1964, 1965, 1987 by The Lockman Foundation.

Scripture quotations marked (NLT) are taken from the Holy Bible, New Living Translation, copyright © 1996, 2004, 2007, 2013, 2015 by Tyndale House Foundation. Used by permission of Tyndale House Publishers, Inc., Carol Stream, Illinois 60188. All rights reserved.

Scripture quotations marked MSG are taken from THE MESSAGE, copyright © 1993, 1994, 1995, 1996, 2000, 2001, 2002 by Eugene H. Peterson. Used by permission of NavPress. All rights reserved. Represented by Tyndale House Publishers, Inc.

Scripture quotations marked (TPT) are taken from The Passion Translation®. Copyright © 2017 by BroadStreet Publishing® Group, LLC. Used by permission. All rights reserved. thePassionTranslation.com.

Scripture quotations marked (EXB) are taken from The Expanded Bible, Copyright © 2011 Thomas Nelson Inc. All rights reserved.

Book design by Treasure Image and Publishing
TreasureImagePublishing.com - 248.403.8046

CONTENTS

Dedication 5

Foreword 7

Nindyl's Testimony 9

Priscilla's Essay 17

Acknowledgments 21

CHAPTER ONE 23
   The Secret Place

CHAPTER TWO 31
   Give Yourself to God

CHAPTER THREE 35
   The Process

CHAPTER FOUR 43
   Forgiveness

CHAPTER FIVE 51
   You Must Stay Balanced

CHAPTER SIX 59
   From the Pit to the Palace

CHAPTER SEVEN 69
Learning How to Listen

CHAPTER EIGHT 77
Don't Blame God for What the Church Does

CHAPTER NINE 85
A Woman of Strength with a Heart of Compassion

CHAPTER TEN 97
God's Love is Always First

CHAPTER ELEVEN 109
Love Is Blind until God Opens Your Eyes

CHAPTER TWELVE 117
Tears of Blood

CONCLUSION 123
By God's Design

DEDICATION

First and foremost, I want to dedicate this book to Almighty God, who is my everything and the source of my life. Thank you so much, Jesus!

And then to my two amazing daughters, of whom I am extremely proud, even when I thought I no longer wanted to live. The thought of my beautiful babies saved my life. Priscilla Abigail Shepack, and Portia Linn Shepack—beside Jesus—you both are the greatest gifts in my life, and I love you both more than words can say.

I also am dedicating this book to my incredible grandson, Justin Martinez Shepack—you are (mean mama's) heart, and I love you so very, very much.

FOREWORD

I met this incredible woman of God years ago, and we became the very best of friends. Nindyl Travers is an amazing woman of God. She has gone through many fires in her life—and yes—her God has brought her through every single one. Through all the trials and tribulations, she has not become bitter—she has become better.

In all the ups and downs of her life, she has only grown closer to her God. Looking back through the many stages of her life—through all the tears, heartache and pain—she has become acutely aware that at every stage, Father God has always had her back. She found that He has been absolutely true to His Word to never leave her or forsake her.

Jesus never left Nindyl's side. Her development as a woman of God depended on her capacity to trust God while she was amid the fire.

All the pages of her book were handwritten by Almighty God—ups and downs, ins and outs, and even the good, the bad, and the ugly. They are all by God's design.

Even what the enemy does in life, God turns around and makes work for our good and to His glory.

This mighty young prophetess wants to share her heart and testimony with the world. I, for one, believe the world needs to hear it. Her burning desire is to show the world the beauty of God's design in the life of every believer, and to win every soul possible to the Lord Jesus Christ.

Nindyl has a gift in design—a God-given ability to see beauty where there is none, and to create beauty for all to enjoy. Her gift of design ranges from home decorating, graphic design, to beauty in makeup. She can clearly see God's design in her own life and yours.

In her book, Nindyl bravely shares her blood, sweat, pain, and tears. Though she walks through the fire, God has given her the unique ability to look back through her life and see that it was all by God's beautiful design.

DR. RAYMOND E. ALLEN, SR. PH.D.
PRESIDENT/FOUNDER OF CHAMPIONS FOR CHRIST INT.
CEO-TRUE TO THE WORD PUBLISHING

NINDYL'S TESTIMONY

Hello, my name is Nindyl Travers, and this is my testimony. I was born in Nicaragua, Central America. When I was a little girl I had everything I ever needed.

I always considered myself a daddy's girl, even though I only saw my dad once a month. Still, that was always the happiest time for me. He gave me anything that I wanted or asked for.

My mom was awesome. She worked hard so that I could have the things I needed in life. I was the fourth child from this particular marriage.

When I was ten years old, my mom left Nicaragua and moved to the United States. I stayed in Nicaragua with my grandparents. They raised me and taught me the principles of life.

When I was seventeen, I came to the United States. This was a huge cultural shock for me and change in my life. I went from being daddy's little princess—having everything in my country—to completely starting over.

I had to adjust to my mom, her new marriage, and my eleven brothers and sisters. This was the reason my mom worked so hard. She felt the burden of providing for all of her children.

My three older siblings and I had to help our mother with house cleaning. I went to school for all of one week. Everything that I have learned, I learned on my own. I wanted to better myself and have a better life.

I am someone that desires to constantly grow and learn. I like to challenge myself and am not one to get complacent in life.

I lived with my mom for about a year before getting married at the age of 19. From this marriage, I gave birth to my two beautiful daughters. However, we divorced after twelve years. Once again, I had to start over.

One year later, I met a man that I truly fell in love with. We married, and he raised my second daughter. He was a great stepfather. We worked together, bought our house together, and everything was great—until I encountered Jesus and accepted Him into my life as my Savior.

I made the decision to be part of a ministry, but I was sick with lots of pain at the time. I lost a lot of weight and doctors couldn't figure out what was wrong with me. I was very depressed. When I went to church, one of the pastors prayed for me.

Whenever I would talk to my husband about the pain, he would tell me that there was nothing wrong with me—but I knew that something was wrong. I shouldn't have been losing so much weight.

I started going to church regularly. Every Sunday when I attended, I would dance and worship God. Every Sunday, my husband would get upset. I believe it was because of the changes that God was causing in my life. He could not understand what was happening. He felt that I had changed ever since I started attending this Christian church. I had faith that God was going to heal me and He did. My husband continued to be upset. We had many arguments because of my going to church and serving in the ministry.

One night, I came from work around 10:00 pm. This was my normal schedule. We argued that night because I found out that he was involved with another woman. The argument escalated and he lost control. He went into the home office, pulled out a gun, and put it to my forehead. It was a loaded automatic. When he put it to my head, I raised my hands and said, "God, I'm all yours."

After I said that, my husband pulled the gun from my head and raised it in the air. I knew at that moment that God had saved my life. I ran to my room and called the police.

My husband followed me. He took the phone from me, asked for my forgiveness and asked me not to call the police. My daughter was there; she had her cell phone and used it to call one of my family members. That family member called the police.

When the police arrived, they arrested my husband and asked me what had happened. They saw the bruises on my legs. I told them that all he did was put the gun up in the air. I was so blindly in love, that I lied and didn't press charges.

He was in jail for three days before I bailed him out. Afterwards, he went to anger management classes. When everything was said and done, we went to court. I told the judge that I was a woman of God and had forgiven him. From there, we stayed together for a few months. My husband pretended that everything was fine, but he left and we eventually filed for divorce. He wanted to keep the house and we went back to court. This was very hard for me.

I continually told him that I loved him, and didn't care about the money. His response was that if I loved him, I would donate everything to him. He said this would also prove to his family how much I loved him.

I was so deeply in love that I believed everything he said. When I went to court, I gave everything to him. I did this—not because of what he told me, but because of the faith that I maintained—and because of my love for God. I realized that God was first in my life. I know that if God weren't in my heart, I probably would have lost my mind. I thank God for allowing different women of God to be there for me when I would cry bitterly.

This is why I share my testimony. There are so many women that are being physically and emotionally abused, who turn to sex, drugs, and alcohol in an effort to deal with their pain, but Jesus is the only one able to heal that pain. I thank God that I found Him because I turned to Him.

God sent angels to protect me and encourage me. He provided me with a job, and I am so grateful. I am a living testimony. God said He would never leave me or forsake me—I am a living testimony to that. I am still here—alive and praising God, loving Him more and more every second of my life. Now, I am in the secret place.

Like most moms, I was checking on my daughter's room to see if it was clean. As I looked around, I saw her essay on top of her dresser—I picked it up because I wanted to know what grade she had received. To my amazement, she had written about one of the worst times in my life, and obviously hers. As I began to read her beautifully written essay, my eyes begin to fill with tears and my heart ached for my precious daughter. I was totally overwhelmed by the pain of my past, but even more overwhelmed by the effects that it had on my baby. She will always be my baby.

I want to share her essay with you; if our story and this book helped even one person, it would have all been worth it.

PRISCILLA'S ESSAY

It was the night before Christmas Eve when spirits are supposed to be jolly, but not in my house. I was in my room watching TV when all I could hear was shouting and screaming. I turned the volume down on the TV remote, so I could hear what was going on. It was my mother and step-dad at the time. My adrenaline began to rise, but I didn't know what to think. Do I just stay in my room? Do I walk out to see what's going on? Any and every possible thought was circling in my head.

I left my room. I just couldn't resist the urge of wanting to see what was going on. I went by this wall where they couldn't see me, but I could see them—I was peeking my head out a little to see them arguing and their angry facial expressions. They were yelling and moving their hands furiously to accentuate how angry they were. Then, I heard, "Go ahead! Hit me," coming from my mom. The tears started to fall.

I ran out the house into an extremely windy and chilly night. I didn't want to go back in the house to hear all the arguing that was taking place. I was outside shivering and crying in the cold not knowing what I should do.

Some time passed, and I went back inside. I saw my mother on the floor and my step-dad. "You see, Priscilla is going to call the police," my mother said. That was the moment I experienced every possible emotion in one. Just looking at my mother's face having a gun to her head, I thought it was all going to be over, I immediately grabbed my phone and ran outside again. I called my sister and told her everything that was happening. I was nervous, worried, and scared. I was scared to call the cops myself, so my sister did it for me.

A few minutes passed and I was still outside on this doleful night. Those bright red and blue lights were flying down the street. The cops saw me outside and stopped their cars right in front of the house.

They told me to go sit in one of their vehicles and so I did. I watched them as they banged on the front door and then eventually kicking it down.

Their guns were out and ready as they ran in the house. The lights were on in the room that my mom and step-dad were in. I was able to see all of the shadows since it was dark outside. Everyone's shadows were moving abruptly fast.

My dad arrived to pick me up because I could not sleep in the house that night, as the cops had ordered. He got out of the car and went towards the house to see what was going on. I saw my step-dad being put in handcuffs from where I was sitting in the cop car. The police walked him to the cop car, put him in, and drove off.

My mom was at the door crying and then came to see me in the police car to tell me that everything will be alright. She gave me a kiss and told me she loved me as she walked me to my dad's car.

My dad got in the car and asked me if I was okay. I waved goodbye to my mom while she was speaking to the police and we drove away.

That night was and will be one I will never forget. The day before Christmas Eve and Christmas was just in two days. Everyone is all excited and in the holiday spirit and then there was me. I just cried almost the whole night, wishing someone would pinch me and wake me up from this nightmare. Then, reality hits and this did all just happen.

After this night, I had to take in that sometimes people just aren't meant to be together, no matter how many years it has been. This definitely has made me wiser. We really never know who our true soul mate is. We never really know anything. Life is just a journey full of mysteries that we will have to find out within time.

ACKNOWLEDGMENTS

First, I want to thank my Lord and Savior, Jesus Christ, and my heavenly Father, almighty God. There have been so many people that God has supernaturally sent my way—personal blessings to my life used by the Holy Spirit to help me in my journey.

I want to say thank you to each one of you. Thank you, thank you, thank you from the bottom of my heart! May God bless you and reward you for all you have done for me, as well as many others. Love you all!

Dr. Raymond E. Allen, Sr.
Dr. David and Angela Burrows
Apostle Reggie and Vera Wilson
Apostle Eugene and Mary Gibson
Apostle James and Denise Gibbs
Pastor Frank and Paris Bailey
Pastors Wade and Shirley Moody

Ronald and Pia Fortune

Pastors Byron and Cindie Bishop

Pastors Zack and Heather Prosser

Pastor Fred and Elizabeth Luter

Denesha Robinson

Janine Bucks

Pastors Jesse and Cathy Duplantis

CHAPTER ONE

The Secret Place

Do you know that God has a secret place where he hides us? Being in this secret place is a beautiful thing; it gets you so close to God that you can hear his heartbeat and gives you the ability to listen to his voice clearly.

A lot of people talk about "The Secret Place" in many different ways. Sometimes, it takes losing everything you have, which is really nothing compared to what you gain in God, because when you have Him, you have the very best. It is truly amazing to have God with you, and in you—actually having God living in you! At this point in my life, I had lost my job, and a lot of friends, and family members etc. When you find yourself at the point that you are losing everything, you begin to ask Him, "What Now?"

So, one thing that you always have to remember is what He says in His word: "I will provide all of your needs."

Philippians 4:6-7
Be anxious for nothing, but in everything by prayer and supplication with thanksgiving, make your request known to God.

So what now?

God had spoken to me 3 years ago about writing this book. I felt I never had the time as a working single mom. He spoke to me again: "You have enough time now for my testimony—for the book." So here I am, writing and sharing my heart for His glory, his kingdom.

The "Secret Place" for some people—it can be "just a prayer-place." But my secret place was a place to die to myself to the point that I just trusted God with everything, knowing that He was in me, and He would never leave me or forsake me (Hebrews 13:5-6).

Sometimes, God brings you back to memories of pain, hard times. Sometimes, He shows you visions of everything that he has done in your life—He shows you what He's doing and what He's going to do. Many times, I don't know how or when He's going to do what He has promised, but one thing I know for sure is that He has me forever … so I trust Him.

I know that he wants my testimony to be public to encourage others. So here I am, dwelling in His secret place with Him, letting Him hold me, love me and protect me and my daughters. The experience of having His love and holding you is the best. His peace is unspeakable.

I had applied for work at a lot of different places, and the doors all seemed closed for me everywhere I applied. But then God says, "The doors that I'm going to open for you, no man can close."

There have been people who have come to me and asked, "What are you going to do?" When they ask, my answer is, "God is going to do it and he is in control. He will open the doors."

I understand now that I need to abide in my secret place—to be able to have the time with Jesus and be obedient to do what He asked me to do.

This book is to testify for His glory and His kingdom to everyone in this world: if He did it for me, He will do it for you ... and He's worthy to be praised.

Chapter One

God's Love ...

My secret place has taught me wisdom and has expanded my knowledge and understanding about God's love. I am so grateful. When you learn to embrace His love, it's truly amazing. I always tell Him: "Father, hold me in your arms and never let me go."

His love is always first. He is a jealous God. Learn to love him more and more each day. Fall deeply in love with Him, knowing that He is the best father and friend that you can ever have. He is the King of Kings and Lord of Lords. There is no other like Him.

God is love, not a business, and not a genie in a bottle. He opened my eyes to see that there are many people who have used His love and name for business reasons for their own personal gain. We have gifts and abilities which are beneficial to our natural living, but there is much wisdom that's required in order to function in our gifts—to express our love of God without drawing people to us for our satisfaction or the fulfillment of our personal agendas.

I have experienced people pimping others' and my gifts via control and manipulation. They have done this so much to many people. God eventually stops the usage of their gifts, which causes them to be non-effective with their own. As a result, they prey on the anointing of the gifts of others.

At first, I was very naïve and wasn't aware they were abusing my gift until I had no money at all, no job and no recourse. Then eventually, they made no phone calls or follow-up to see about me, or to say "How are you?" or "Can I get you anything?" My eyes are opened now, because I had to see it myself.

I asked myself the question: "Is this God ... the way they operate? When you give them $1,000 every month, everybody loves you ... but then when you lose your job, no one calls to check on you to see if you're ok?"

God spoke to me saying, "No one ever is going to love you like I do, so don't put your trust in man, just trust me. I am your Father, your Provider ... I'm your everything." He said, "Call upon me, not on flesh."

It was at this point that I realized how important it is not to blame God or charge Him foolishly for what man was doing. People are always going to be people, but God's love will always remain the same.

So, what is God's Love? God's love is a one-on-one relationship, not a religion.

When you go to your secret place and you realize that there is no one like God, you encounter God's personal, intimate love for you. It draws you to get on your knees on a regular basis, call on His name and ask Him to give you His strength. Then, you can continue to move forward knowing that the army of God, the angels, and the fire of the Holy Spirit will go before you and protect you.

God's love is completely all-consuming in my Secret Place; I've learned to Love God more and allow Him to love me back.

CHAPTER TWO

Give Yourself to God

Though there are many different reasons to give, the best reason to give is the love. If God never did another thing for us, we still would never be able to catch up with all He has given us.

When we do give, we must be sure we are following the leading of the Holy Spirit. Many times we give from the motivation of emotion.

At the beginning, when I first came to the ministry, I was sensitive in my spirit and very cheerful about giving out of love, and out of my heart for everyone in need. I would go to people sitting in the congregation and I slip a monetary seed into their hand discretely because I wanted it to be between me and God. This carried on for a period of four years of my life. I was fortunate to remain faithful in my tithes and offerings.

I soon began visiting different ministries and I began to take the best teachings from them including Love and Respect for everyone. I planted a seed into each of the ministries I visited, expecting nothing in return except love, which is what God is. God is Love.

In every ministry that I visited, I learned how to love everyone there and they love me. I still continue to visit and support them, but now it's time for my ministry to launch. This is the reason why I came to the secret place; but I gave everything to God—my whole heart, life, soul, and spirit belong to Him.

Some people say you have to hit rock bottom in order to progress. I know I needed time to meditate so that my Father could speak to me clearly. He spoke to me saying: "My daughter, it's time for your ministry."

You can never skip the process. Though you want to make it easy, it's not easy. Sometimes you even want to walk away from the call, but God puts you back in.

Chapter Two

When He has picked you, you can't run from it. You do have a free will. But loving Him like I do, I can't resist Him; in fact, I gravitate towards Him. There may be tears of blood, or tears of pain, but at the same time there will be tears of joy. There is unspeakable joy when you feel him holding you in His arms, never letting go.

I always ask Him, "Lord, hold me in your arms and never let me go." It was an intimate, one-on-one conversation. I am so grateful for Him holding me, holding my babies, and letting me see that even though I may lose my job, or material things, I could have the peace that passes all understanding.

I could have the joy in knowing that He's going to take care of everything. How? I can't say, except "you know that you know" that He's got it. He's the only one who can perform the miracles and wonders. He's the only one who can open every door; who can bring you up and put you higher.

After everything I have gone through, people still ask me, "How are you doing it?" I reply saying, "I'm not doing anything—my Father's doing it." Normally, they smile and say, "Who's your father?" Then I smile back and say, "The King of Kings—the best one—God Almighty."

CHAPTER THREE

The Process

 My daughter, all I've been doing is molding you to my design. Everything that you have gone through was part of the process so that you would be able to testify, help and encourage others which would allow you to stand up *straight in confidence like a queen and declare: I am God's design—his daughter.*

He created and molded me for His kingdom and for His Glory. That's why I love him, praise Him, and glorify his Holy name.

There were times when I would go places and pray for people, and God would allow me to see and feel things via the gift that he's placed within me. To keep it real, at times I would even ask God, "Please don't let me see this ... I don't want to see that anymore," because I was tired and trying to give up.

Then He'd say, "You are my vessel of whom I have chosen to pray for them." I answered, "Lord I surrender—I'm all yours." I would end up praying for people who needed it and release the word that he wanted to release.

It was awesome the way that God moved—people would cry tears of joy rendering big smiles, kissing me, hugging me and telling me thank you. I'd say, "Don't thank me; thank our Father in heaven, Jesus, our God, our King. He is the one who used me to perform miracles, and he is the one I glorify." Then I would grab their hand, and together we thanked God and glorified His name.

When you're in the process, you may become tired and drained because you help and pray for so many people. That's the very reason you need to fellowship with God's people. They will lift you up and encourage you to go on.

It is also important that you have a day for rest. Do what you can do to be at peace—go to the park or lake to get away. Dwell in God's presence so that He can hold you and recharge you, by giving you the strength to get up and do it over and over again. Your work is to serve Him and be His vessel in obedience. Constantly surrender yourself to Him, and do all things that He says and instructs you to do. Pray for the people He leads you to—whether they are sick, struggling in pain or despair—whether they reside in your homeland or foreign lands. Pray for them all in love, speaking life always, neglecting none of them.

Please understand that when you pray, you have to speak life. This is very important because when you call someone, they may pray about various things such as vengeance, pettiness, or trivialness—you must recognize that this is not God to pray this way. God is life, love, peace, grace, and mercy.

This can be confusing sometimes for some people who are praying out of their hurt or emotions, but you'll identify the heart and will of God with your prayers—God will confirm it within your spirit when you feel the fire of the Holy Spirit, and you'll know it's nothing but God. You have an assurance that whatever is spoken to you will come to pass.

In the process, you will go through a lot. Sometimes, gifted people will pray for you. However, they may tell you "I will pray for you but I need you to get me "this or that" ... moneywise.

See, when someone wants to pray for you, it has to be from the heart. There should not be any money involved. If you want to plant a seed at your own will, freedom or unction, then that is a separate issue. You should never feel manipulated or controlled into sowing into (or paying) someone, especially for ministerial purposes. When someone asks you for money because they need to pray for you, that is not God.

Once again, I went through all of this and it took me a while to understand. But I learned that God is love and if somebody is doing God's work, it is their motivation has to be love. If you decide to give a gift, it's up to you, but you should never feel obligated just because they pray for you. God is not a business.

When I first came into faith, I encountered so much manipulation, but now that I am standing by God's word. There is no part of me that will pray for you, asking for money back. My spirit does not agree with or like that. I don't want anyone else to go through what I went through. I want you to understand that it has to be from your heart—not your emotion—if you want to give something to somebody. But you don't just <u>have</u> to.

God never asked you for anything to receive his love. His real love is not for sale.

When I love somebody, my love is not for sale. Neither is my gift that God has given me for sale. I don't do God's love for business. God's love is love, and His gift to you is to be able to give freely to everyone who needs his love—not sell it.

Be wise about who is around you. There are too many people who just want to take and take and take. There are many dream and vision-stealers as well. For instance—you share an idea you have for a vision of your own, then they turn around and get it done behind your back—only to bring it back in your face with a smile, knowing that it was your idea all along.

So you look back and say: "Lord has this really happened? Has this really happened? This is it?"

This is real life. Some people have a pure heart, but then some people have a heart that has a few problems in it. God needs to work in their heart, clean it up and give them a new heart. He normally does this when you accept Christ as your Savior.

So, I want to encourage you to be careful. You can't trust everybody. You have to love and trust God first, then love and trust yourself.

God will send angels—His messengers—to your life. You can recognize them by asking God through prayer, "What is it about this person? Are you sending them to me, or are they coming for other reasons?" If they are not coming from God, you can stop them in the name of Jesus, by the Blood of Jesus, with the power of the Holy Spirit. Stop it in the mighty name of Jesus! When you use that authority, God will remove them out of the way because they are not for you.

There are also people who come into our life just for a season. Throughout the various seasons in my life, I've had a lot of people to come in and out of my life. It took me a while to understand that some were only for a season. I may still talk to them or say "Hi." Even though I still love them and want to keep some in my life, God reminds me that they were in my life for a limited time that He has orchestrated and predestined. When that season is completed, it is time to let go.

Father GOD I'm Praying for

FORGIVENESS

"For if you forgive men when they sin against you, your heavenly Father will also forgive you. But, if you do not forgive men their sins, your Father will not forgive your sins."
(Mat 6:14-15)

CHAPTER FOUR

Forgiveness

Luke 6:27-28 (KJV)
But I say unto you which hear, Love your enemies, do good to them which hate you, bless them that curse you, and pray for them which despitefully use you.

Sometimes when you go through pain, you feel like you just don't know what to do. "How can I forgive this person who has done me so much wrong?"

What do you do? How do you deal with that, because it's really disappointing? You put your expectation in a human instead of God. You think God is going to change people—and He does change people—but sometimes it takes a while for them to understand or want to be changed. Nine times out of ten God really wants to change you.

Thank you, Jesus, because even though we don't deserve anything, you still forgive us!

When people are hurt by others, some people get angry, others get quiet, and some just cry—but deep inside there is that constant pain of disappointment in their heart.

What do you do when you feel you have done everything for a person, and you are disappointed? All you can say is, "Lord, how could it be possible for there to be so much pain in my heart?"

You may even say "I forgive them," but you don't forget what they've done. When that happens, it means is that you really haven't released everything to God—so, it keeps coming back and attacking you again and again. You get depressed and cry because you're disappointed, which is normal because you're human. But you cannot stay wandering around that disappointment.

Chapter Four

Remember how the children of Israel kept going around and around in circles in the wilderness? An 11 day journey took the Israelites 40 years, (Joshua 5:6)! God could not bring them into the promise land because they refused to learn the lesson He was trying to teach them.

The only thing you can do is look up to heaven and say, "Lord I can't carry this disappointment anymore. I'll give it all to you. I surrender my total will to you Lord. I've tried to do everything with love, therefore I should not be affected; I should be protected with regards to this pain …" Then, remember what they did to Jesus at the cross—His final words were, "Father, forgive them for they know not what they do."

Sometimes, when you have done good things from a sincere heart and you become offended or disappointed, there is a little process that you go through. You may ask, "God, Father, how could you allow this to happen when I am trying to do everything from my heart with love?" He will remind you what He went through, and you'll stand up and say, "Lord, if they did it to you, doesn't mean they're not going to do it to me. I'm just going to stand up with a smile on my face, and I forgive them, I release them," then you can forget and let it go.

Just like they say, "Let Go and let God." This is so important because it's not good to have pain weighing on your soul. It is best for you to let go and truly forgive. Forgiveness is not as much for the people who hurt you as it is for you.

People ask me, "How can I just forgive somebody with all of the mistreatment I've gone through? How, can I forgive them? How can I forgive the people who keep coming and taking and taking and taking, but not giving back?"

I've always been a giving person—to the point that I didn't have anything, (but I actually have everything because I have Jesus! I'm rich in my heart, my spirit, my soul my mind, and in the Holy Spirit. I'm rich from how my Father has blessed me, because I'm alive I'm a grateful person, so I praise Him).

Chapter Four

I always respond, "How? You have to love them with the love of God. You really have to love them, because if you don't love them, it will be hard for you to forgive and forget." In my heart I pray, "Lord, I just don't want them to do the same thing to other people—how can I stop it?"

Here is the secret: You cannot stop it because you are not God. God is the only one who has the power to stop these things. Sometimes it takes time to get to the point and understand that you are not God—you cannot carry everybody.

I went through that, I tried to carry a lot of people. I didn't want to let them go because of my good and pure heart, and because of that I went through disappointments.

I asked God: "How do you take this disappointment away? How do I get it out so I don't feel the pain anymore?" His answer was, "Forgive them, daughter. You did what you were supposed to do. You did it from love; therefore it's up to them to do what they're supposed to do, not you. You're already done."

So, I prayed, "Father, thank you for allowing me to forgive them and forget. Thank you for giving me a new fresh and pure heart that's filled with fresh love every day, just like to fill me with strength. You're just so awesome."

When you allow God's love to strengthen you, then it really doesn't matter what people say or do. Some people may tell you, "Where is your God?" They'll make fun of you or they'll think you're crazy. They did it to me, they did it to Jesus—what makes you think they're not going to do it to you?

Having a sensitive spirit, it was hard for me to pass through this test of disappointment and unforgiveness, not because I was upset with them. I would still talk to them, I'd still love them, but that little disappointment was there. I asked God to change my sensitive heart; His response was, "I won't change your heart. I made it that way, that's why I picked you."

I began praying for those who hurt me, "Please Heavenly Father, don't let them do that to other people.

Chapter Four

Please talk to them, Jesus. Let them see so they don't hurt anyone else."

You know, I understand that God is love, and I understand that He forgives us. I understand that we disappoint Him sometimes and we get angry. When we get angry, all we can do is ask God to forgive us, repent, and he will fill us up with love.

When it is hard for you to forgive, remember how much God forgives us again and again; and if God forgives us, why not you? Why would you not forgive? You're going to live your life miserable and grumpy. You won't be a happy person with peace in your heart.

See, you don't want to do that. You want to be able to do the opposite. You want to be happy, rejoice, sing, praise, dance, and jump up and down—whatever you want to do—living in the freedom of forgiveness!

I give all the credit and honor to God. I'm just a woman, I'm not perfect—I'm just a woman like everyone else. In my life, God has done everything that I had done—blessing people, praying for people, loving people, forgiving people and continuing to support one another, love and help one another.

I'm just happy that I can actually share this with anyone in the world. Don't carry the disappointment and hate in your heart because all it's going to do is damage you on the inside—it's not worth it. The best thing you can do is forgive and forget what happened and let God deal with it. Let God talk to them.

You can choose to put a smile on your face. When anyone asks you: "How can you be so happy?" Let your answer be, "God, God lives in me, and He's with me all my life. So, I am so grateful!"

Thank you, Lord, for forgiving our sins and sacrificing your life for us. Even though we didn't deserve it, we are grateful for what you have done for us. So, I say thank you, my Lord, Thank you, my Father. You are the King of Kings, and this is for your kingdom. I give Honor and glory to your name, Jesus. Amen.

CHAPTER FIVE

You Must Stay Balanced

Being balanced in your walk for God is vitally important. It keeps you centered and protects you from becoming too extreme in one direction or another.

I have a dear friend, Dr. Raymond E. Allen, Sr., who graduated from Rhema Bible College in 1980, which was the last year you could go to Rhema for one year and receive a diploma. It was called the Year of Balance.

Here are some scriptures that show us the importance of being balanced.

> ***Ecclesiastes 3:1-8 (KJV)***
> *To every thing there is a season, and a time to every purpose under the heaven: a time to be born, and a time to die; a time to plant, and a time to pluck up that which is planted; a time to kill, and a time to heal; a time to break down, and a time to build up; a time to weep, and a time to laugh; a time to mourn, and a time to dance; a time to cast away stones, and a time to gather stones together; a time to embrace, and a time to refrain from embracing; a time to get, and a time to lose; a time to keep, and a time to cast away;*

a time to rend, and a time to sew; a time to keep silence, and a time to speak; a time to love, and a time to hate; a time of war, and a time of peace.

Ecclesiastes 7:16 (KJV)
Be not righteous over much; neither make thyself over wise: why shouldest thou destroy thyself?

Ecclesiastes 7:16 (AMP)
Do not be excessively righteous [like those given to self-conceit], and do not be overly wise (pretentious)—why should you bring yourself to ruin?

As you can see, balance is good. Think of the discipline and effort a gymnast has to have in order to master the balance beam. She does all kind of various moves—she prances, leaps, does a back handspring, and even a pirouette—but the one thing that is vital above all, which she can never forget, is to stay balanced.

It is the very same with us in our walk for the Lord Jesus Christ. No matter what moves we make, no matter what we are going though at the time, we must always stay centered in God; we must always remain balanced.

Keeping Your Balance When Going Through Pain

Though I was going through pain, I still would get up in the morning and get ready. I tried never to show the pain because I had faith.

God would always strengthen me. I would look in the mirror to get ready, and He'd tell me, "Get ready Nindyl. Get ready. You have to go. You've got to keep moving Nindyl. You've gotta do this for your daughters." I'm a single mother, and I have to get it done. It was really tough.

On my days off, I relax and cry out at my house. When it was time to work, I'd go with a happy face and smile, leaving my problems at home so that I could properly handle business at work.

Now, I'm talking about a job, not my work for my Father. My work for my Father is what I can do 24/7. At times, this consisted of people calling me throughout the night to ask me for prayer. I was always available, never saying "No" because these were people who never told me "NO".

Balance allows me to be transparent with newcomers through doing God's work of motivating and encouraging them to do better—not limiting them to their shortcomings. It is always good to be nice to newcomers, without any pressure through greeting and introducing yourself to them and embracing them into the family of Christ. It is important that we invite them to attend services on a regular basis so that they can experience the wholesomeness of God through the assembly of the brethren of His kingdom.

Through the process of fellowship, and attending church, we hear the Word of God, which brings constant balance to our lives.

We should also remain in touch with them with a follow-up call at least once a week, to help them establish themselves in the soils and environment of their new life—showing them that their presence in the ministry is not based on the money or resources that they can bring.

For instance, in love, we can teach them the spiritual fundamentals of giving based on the scriptures. This way, they can feel and see that we are about the love of God and His Kingdom; it's God's church, not man's church. Jesus said the Kingdom of God is within you—it is in your heart. Once the kingdom and His church is in your heart, you can produce fruit by winning souls to Christ.

Hebrews 10:24-25 (KJV)
And let us consider one another to provoke unto love and to good works: not forsaking the assembling of ourselves together, as the manner of some is; but exhorting one another: and so much the more, as ye see the day approaching.

We should all endeavor to develop and maintain balance in all things because God is a God of balance and order.

1 Corinthians 14:40
Let all things be done decently and in order. (KJV)
But all things must be done appropriately and in an orderly manner. (AMP)

But all things should be done with regard to decency and propriety and in an orderly fashion. (AMPC)

But let everything be done in a ·right [proper; fitting] and orderly way. (EXB)

All things should be done in the right way, one after the other. (NLV)

... doing all things in a beautiful and orderly way. (TPT)

This passage of scripture really reveals a lot about God, it says that God wants us to do all things in decency and in order—this speaks to balance. God is telling us this because this is how he operates. God is a God of balance. Being balanced helps you do everything decently and in order.

It Is So Important To Be Spiritually Balanced

- Because God is a God of Balance and Order
- It will keep you from destruction
- It will keep you from becoming religious
- Truth is a balancer/ The Word is truth

Truth is a balancer, or we could say the Word of God is a balancer. This is really important. The main reason we study the Word of God is so that we can live an effective life in Christ.

Psalm 119:130 (KJV)
The entrance of thy words giveth light; it giveth understanding unto the simple.

Psalm 119:11 (KJV)
Thy word have I hid in mine heart, that I might not sin against thee.

We're studying the Word of God so that we can discover who He is, and live an effective life in Christ. If we allow God's Holy Word to rule in our lives, it will cause us to be balanced. His Word will help guide and direct our lives on the path of righteousness. Praise God!

I want to encourage you today, dear hearts—children of the Most High God—to stay on the beam! Stay balanced and don't fall off. If you happened to fall off the spiritual balance beam, then get back up in Jesus Name!

CHAPTER SIX

From the Pit to the Palace

I remember the great seasons in my life so far—times when I was up, and times when I was down. My mind was running out of control, and I even felt I wanted to die. I was in the pit of despair. It felt like I was all alone in this world with no one to watch over me.

You know, I really believe that the greatest times we can demonstrate our love and faith in God is when we are in the pit—or the lion's den, or our fiery furnace! God is always watching. He is really always with us.

One of my all-time favorite characters in the Bible is Joseph, the dreamer (Genesis 37). Have you ever had someone hate you because of the dream God gave you? It was like they drank a whole bottle of *Haterade* ... you know exactly who I'm talking about.

Well, Joseph had his haters—and, it just so happened that they were his brothers. They hated him so much because he was his father's favorite son. The father showed him partiality—even giving him a coat of many colors.

Chapter Six

It all seemed to be going well for Joseph until one day, out of nowhere, he found himself looking up from the pit! He went from being the favorite son to being a slave. This had to be a shock for the favorite son.

Let's go visit Joseph in the pit:

Genesis 37:20-27 (KJV)

Come now therefore, and let us slay him, and cast him into some pit, and we will say, Some evil beast hath devoured him: and we shall see what will become of his dreams. And Reuben heard it, and he delivered him out of their hands; and said, Let us not kill him. And Reuben said unto them, Shed no blood, but cast him into this pit that is in the wilderness, and lay no hand upon him; that he might rid him out of their hands, to deliver him to his father again.

And it came to pass, when Joseph was come unto his brethren, that they stript Joseph out of his coat, his coat of many colours that was on him; and they took him, and cast him into a pit: and the pit was empty, there was no water in it. And they sat down to eat bread: and they lifted up their eyes and

> *looked, and, behold, a company of Ishmeelites came from Gilead with their camels bearing spicery and balm and myrrh, going to carry it down to Egypt. And Judah said unto his brethren, What profit is it if we slay our brother, and conceal his blood? Come, and let us sell him to the Ishmeelites, and let not our hand be upon him; for he is our brother and our flesh. And his brethren were content.*

As you can clearly see their intent was to kill Joseph. (Somebody say, "But God!") Thank God for the Reubens in our lives!

Notice, they stripped Joseph out of his coat of many colors. When the enemy hates you, his desire is to kill, steal, and destroy—removing the coat was like taking his authority, removing his status, and removing his favor, (or so they thought).

You see, Joseph's secret was that he was not just favored by his father; Joseph was favored by The Father—Almighty God. Joseph went from being betrayed by his brothers and thrown in a pit to reigning in the palace of Pharaoh in Egypt.

Chapter Six

Joseph was the greatest type or picture of Jesus our Savior found in the Old Testament. As you study the life of both Jesus and Joseph, you will see they had many similarities. Joseph is a picture of Jesus—and just like Jesus, Joseph had to go down before he went up.

Many of us will praise and worship God when we are in the palace, but how many will keep giving God praise when you are in the pit?

When you have no friends in the pit and it seems like all have forsaken you? There is loneliness, rejection and anger in the pit. We can even throw in a "Why Me?" in the pit.

But praise God Almighty! He promised never to leave me or forsake me. Jesus said He with be with me until the end of the age.

You know just when it seemed like it could get no worst, Joseph went from the pit to slavery, and then from slavery to prison. But even in his hardship, God was there with him—in the pit, in slavery, and in prison.

Psalm 30:5 declares, "Weeping may endure for a night, but joy comes in the morning." I remember telling someone weeping may only endure for a night, but in some parts of the world, the night can last for 6 months. But the night does not last forever, and seasons always change.

Joseph's gift and his anointing finally made room for him, and the time came when he was brought before Pharaoh. He went from the pit to the palace. When he got to the palace, the gift of visions, dreams and favor went right with him. He endured the suffering, but God exalted him in due season. The palace was right where God wanted him all along.

When you go through trials, keeping your faith in God, you gain God's wisdom and insight. You understand that you can't take hatred with you to the palace. You can't take vengeance with you to the palace. You can't take strife and bitterness with you to the palace. These things hinder your growth, and keep you bound in prison.

Joseph was so happy to see his brothers that he wept and held them tight in his arms. He loved them dearly, and all the past was forgotten—it was no more. Joseph realized that God had sent him to Egypt—not only to save his family, but to save the entire nation of Israel. Glory to God!

> ***Genesis 45:4-7 (KJV)***
>
> *And Joseph said unto his brethren, Come near to me, I pray you. And they came near. And he said, I am Joseph your brother, whom ye sold into Egypt. Now therefore be not grieved, nor angry with yourselves, that ye sold me hither: for God did send me before you to preserve life. For these two years hath the famine been in the land: and yet there are five years, in the which there shall neither be earing nor harvest. And God sent me before you to preserve you a posterity in the earth, and to save your lives by a great deliverance.*

Even though Joseph's trials were many, his position changed in one day (Genesis 41)! Suddenly, he went from being a prisoner to being a co-ruler with Pharaoh. In a moment, he was given a position of authority and honor in the palace. I want to tell you today that, no matter what the situation or how long you have been in your circumstance, God can give you a right-now miracle!

You may be are in that pit season right now. Trust God! He sees you and He loves you. He has not forgotten you.

I remember having a loaded gun pointed at my head by the man I loved most in the world. I just knew with everything within me that I was about to die. I raised my hands, and scream out at the top of my lungs "Lord I'm all Yours," and instantly he removed the gun. That was a part of my pit season. I knew God had saved my life! "Won't He Do It!!!"

Right now, I want to stop here and pray for the women in the world that have suffered abuse. If that includes you, I want you to know that you don't deserve that treatment—it's not your fault. It really hurts the heart of God when you constantly blame yourself, put yourself down, and when you don't see how beautiful you really are.

Chapter Six

I cover you right now, with the precious blood of Jesus. I speak directly to the situation and the spirit that's driving that abuse and command it to leave. I bind it by the authority of Almighty God, and the mighty name of Jesus—the Name above all names. Be Free now, in Jesus mighty name! You deserved to be loved, honored, cherished, and adored ... Amen.

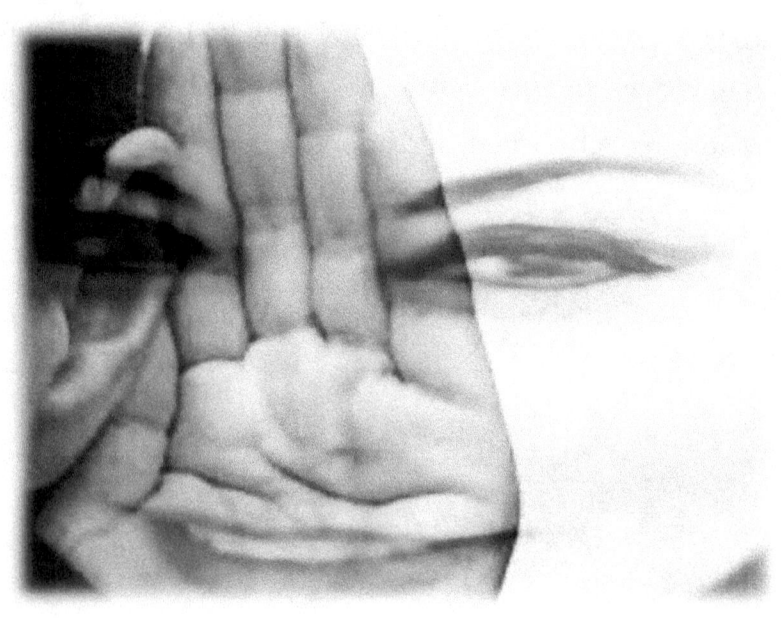

CHAPTER SEVEN

Learning How to Listen

There is a gift that I feel has really been neglected by so many people—it is the art of listening. This is so important in ministry, in relationships, and especially in regards to God. The Word of God has a lot to say about listening or hearing.

> *James 1:19 (KJV)*
> *Wherefore, my beloved brethren, let every man be swift to hear, slow to speak, slow to wrath ...*

> *Luke 2:46 (KJV)*
> *And it came to pass, that after three days they found him in the temple, sitting in the midst of the doctors, both hearing them, and asking them questions.*

> *Matthew 13:9 (KJV)*
> *Who hath ears to hear, let him hear.*

> *John 10:27 (KJV)*
> *My sheep hear my voice, and I know them, and they follow me ...*

> *Matthew 13:16 (KJV)*
> *But blessed are your eyes, for they see: and your ears, for they hear.*

We see several things regarding listening from the above passages of scripture. Listening is vital, not only to your personal relationships, but to your spiritual relationship to God.

One of the problems of being overly religious or caught up in what I call the *"religious matrix"* is that it makes it impossible for you to truly hear God—even though you may think you got it going on!

Jesus identified the religious by their tendency to <u>not</u> His Words. He said that if you are really a part of Him, you would receive His Words. But He hid His Word from those who weren't His. This is why He spoke in parables.

> *Matthew 13:10-13 (KJV)*
> *And the disciples came, and said unto him, Why speakest thou unto them in parables? He answered and said unto them, Because it is given unto you to know the mysteries of the kingdom of heaven, but to them it is not given. For whosoever hath, to him shall be given, and he shall have more abundance: but whosoever hath not, from him shall be taken away even that he hath. Therefore speak I to them in parables: because they seeing see not; and hearing they hear not, neither do they understand.*

God's wisdom and insight was only for those who were a part of Christ kingdom. He said "hearing they hear not and seeing they see not, neither do they understand." Another way of saying this is that even though they see, they refuse to accept what they are seeing; they hear but refuse to embrace His words because of their religion.

If you are sitting in a classroom with the greatest teacher in the Universe, but someone has you blindfolded and also has your ears plugged so that you can hear nothing, how much understanding are you going to get? How much will you learn? Absolutely nothing!

As parents, we tell our children, "Can you just listen please?" You know their brains are going all over the place so it's kind of hard for them to listen sometimes. You just keep repeating and repeating it until they finally understand it. Well, sometimes as an adult, we go through the same thing.

It's kind of hard to even learn how to stay quiet because you're so excited that you just accepted Jesus Christ as your Savior, and you're so excited about all your new experiences. You are constantly asking questions, and you never really take time to sit down and just listen. It was so hard for me, but in time, I learned to just listen.

But here's the funny part: A lot of pastors, prophetesses, and friends of mine are older than me, and they were teaching me saying, "Nindyl, learn how to listen. You should never say I know—I know—I know. You should just stay quiet and listen."

It is important to hear their wisdom because they know more than us, and they have experienced more than us—they are spiritual mothers and fathers in the ministry. They have been there for a long time, and they have fruit that remains. So listen, and stay quiet.

This was a challenge for me because I always wanted to talk. Now that I have experienced life in God and I have grown, I understand what they were saying. Now, I'm talking to people and it's my time to teach and share wisdom. When I'm trying to teach people who don't listen or pay attention, I want to say, "Don't you want to learn? Do you want this or do you not want this? Do you really want to pay attention, or do you want to call me with the same issue next week that you're having this week?"

Listening is awesome—it really is a ministry of its own. Sometimes when we listen, we can actually feel the people's heart. Let them talk. Just make the decision, "I'm just going to listen today." Just stay quiet and listen and watch what the Holy Spirit will do. It's going to be awesome.

When you start learning, you'll understand why your spiritual mothers and fathers were telling you that. Then you'll think, "Wow! Thank you Lord for sending those people into my life … and now here I am, listening to them because they encourage me."

Now in this phase of my life, I'm trying to do what they did, and I understand what they talk about. Listening is very important. It's one of the most powerful tools given to us in ministry, and when you learn to master the art of listening, you will see many hearts healed, and many lives changed for the glory of the Lord.

Proverbs 20:12 (KJV)
The hearing ear, and the seeing eye, the Lord hath made even both of them.

Take time to listen to the voice of God. Sometimes you're so busy, going all over the place, and God just wants you to just stop and listen. "You are working my work. You are supposed to be just listening to my word and my voice—not all over. You really can't concentrate like that." God can be just talking to you and you'll be so busy or scattered, you'll miss it. Be very careful with that.

It's just like when parents tell their kids: "Can you hear me?" Well, they know they can hear because they got those two big-old ears up-side their head! When the parents say, "Did you hear me?" they are saying that because the children did not give the proper reaction to what was said.

Hearing is obedience. In the New Testament, (which was written in Greek) the word for *hear* it also means *obey*. They go hand in hand. God sometimes tells us: "Can you hear me?" What he's trying to tell us is: "Can you hear me and obey what you hear?" You have to be really attentive to listen to His voice so that you can function better in your work.

Please remember, God gave you one mouth, and two ears! You ought to be doing twice as much listening as you do talking.

Romans 10:17 (KJV)
So then faith cometh by hearing, and hearing by the word of God.

Hearing is a key to your faith. It is so important that without hearing you cannot have faith, and without faith. Hebrews 11:6 says "It's impossible to please God." Real faith comes by hearing and hearing by the Word of God.

Proverbs 4:20-22 (KJV)
My son, attend to my words; incline thine ear unto my sayings. Let them not depart from thine eyes; keep them in the midst of thine heart. For they are life unto those that find them, and health to all their flesh.

Be very careful how you listen, but at the same time be very careful at what (and who) you're listening to. If it's not the Word of the living God, which gives life, then eat the meat and spit out the bones.

Shhhhh ... Be very quiet. Can you hear that? Listen very closely ... do you hear it now? It's the longing hearts of untold millions of people crying out for God. It's time God's people to start listening as never before ... Praise God!

CHAPTER EIGHT

Don't Blame God for What the Church Does

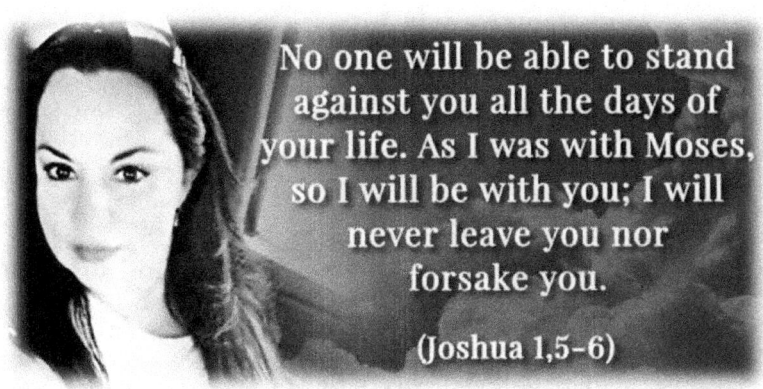

> No one will be able to stand against you all the days of your life. As I was with Moses, so I will be with you; I will never leave you nor forsake you.
>
> (Joshua 1,5-6)

This subject is very close to my heart because of the things I suffered at the hands of "the church." However, I want you to understand that when we talk about the church, we have to very careful—the true church is the actual living body of Christ in the earth. So many times we say "the church" when we actually mean certain individuals in the church.

Now that we've got that straight, let's continue.

When I was new to church, I came in with such new passion and excitement. I loved to give—often I would give beyond my means because I didn't know any better. Many times, I was actually taken advantage of by those in the church system that I had trusted.

We really need to understand this: whenever people are involved in a thing, there is going to be a tendency towards error, because humans are imperfect.

Just because a man or woman is one of God's servant does not mean they are infallible; they can make mistakes, and they can miss the mark. It does not even mean they don't love God. You can have the greatest heart in the world and still make a mistake. We all do!

I want to give you a principle that will really help safeguard you, protect your heart, and keep your mind from deception. God's living Word has provided safeguards to help us.

Matthew 7:16 tells us you can tell a tree by the fruit it bears. Anytime you are dealing with a person or ministry "just follow the fruit." If the fruit is godly, righteous, holy, and pure, then you know it's a good ministry.

God has given us the ability to discern right from wrong based on his Word. His Word is the final authority for all things. It tells us how to walk, how to talk, and how to carry ourselves in the ministry. It even tells us how to think!

He has told us to test the spirits by His Spirit. If right now we were to open a church for all those "wounded by the church," we would have the largest congregation in the United States.

There are times when your anger and pain may be justified. However, instead of taking it to the Lord in prayer, are you being like Adam, running and hiding from God? What has God ever done but love you and provide for you? He only wants the very best for us in all areas of life. What did Jesus ever do to you, but love you so much that he willingly died for you?

Please stop blaming God for what people have done in His name. God is not responsible for anything but loving you.

The true church is to be a refuge, a place of healing and deliverance, a place of peace and safety. It's a hospital for the mind, soul, and body. A place of love, joy, and constant edification where God's people can find everything they need to help them grow and develop in the fullness of God.

Hebrews 10:24-25 (KJV)
And let us consider one another to provoke unto love and to good works: not forsaking the assembling of ourselves together, as the manner of some is; but exhorting one another: and so much the more, as ye see the day approaching.

Many marvelous things happen in a church where the Word of God is honored. In the house of God, believers are instructed in righteousness, and ministered to in a myriad of ways. It is a place of community and powerful support. God's house is the ultimate place for answers, vision, and encouragement.

When Jesus Christ resurrected from Abraham's Bosom, he gave gifts unto men for the perfecting of the saints. The gifts he gave are gifts of ministry, apostles, prophets, evangelists, pastors, and teachers (Ephesians 4:8-12). The primary anchor for these ministry gifts to operate is the formal church setting. The benefits of congregating in God's house are more than I could number.

Isn't the power that is in the church amazing! God commands us not to forsake the assembling of ourselves together, as the manner of some is, but exhorting one another: and so much the more as you see that evil day approaching. It is telling us that as times get worse, we have a shelter in the Church of the living God. Believers are supposed to come together to bless each other and exhort and encourage one another. We draw power from our unity in the faith.

In Matthew 18:20, Jesus declares "Where two or more are gathered together I am in the midst." Even though I know there are many believers that stay at home and get all their teaching from television, that was never God's plan. It's all about interaction, coming together and blessing each other in Jesus' Name. We are to fellowship.

In today society, there has really been an apparent disconnect from personal relationships. Because of technology, everyone seems to end up in their own private little world. For example, I was at a restaurant one time, and I saw a large family out eating dinner together. As I watched them, I noticed they were all on their phones. Their table was super quiet—there was no interaction, no laughter, and no eye contact with each other. It was like they were all possessed by the almighty power of the cell phone.

My ex-husband hated the fact that I got saved and did not like me going to church, but I risked everything and gave my all to the church—my time, my finances, everything—I even almost lost my life. So, now that I am free to go to the house of the Lord, it is such a beautiful feeling. I attend Pastors Jesse and Cathy Duplantis' church. The Word is reviving and restoring my soul. It is a beautiful experience to have pastors who really love their people. It is truly amazing. They are true pastors in every sense of the word.

Now, what happens when you are hurt by a person (even a pastor) in the church? Did you know every time you have the opportunity to get offended, the devil has set a trap for you to fall in? The word *offense* in the New Testament is the Greek word *"Skandalon,"* which is the part of the trap that the bait is placed on. When you take the bait of offense, the trap slams shut and you are trapped!

A lot of times, these individuals don't even realize they have hurt or offended you. But because you're hurt, you run off, hopping from church to church, leaving a long trail of offenses and broken relationships—or you stop going to church altogether because you are mad at God for what someone else did.

If you are reading this right now, and you know you have been offended by the church, then broke up with God—I want you to look deep into your heart, and forgive the individuals that offended you. Please say this confession prayer with me, I believe God is going to set you free in Jesus' Name.

Dear Lord, in the mighty and matchless name of Jesus Christ, we release those that have hurt us or offended in any way. Jesus, we will not blame you for what people have done—whether in the church or out of the church—we release everyone. Father, we forgive them. I know that unless I forgive, you cannot and forgive me. I forgive because you forgave me of all my sins. Today, Father, I repent. I ask forgiveness for myself. I will return to your house, the place of blessings that bears your name. I will return to church to be blessed, but more so to be a blessing. I will return to church because your Word tells me not to forsake the assembling of ourselves together. I need the church, and they need me. Today is my day to be free. Today is my day of liberation. Father, I will never ever again blame you for what man has done.

CHAPTER NINE

A Woman of Strength with a Heart of Compassion

In the world we live in today, there is a contention between man and woman—almost like man vs. woman mentality. However, when you understand God's original plan, the male and female are called to rule and reign together. Each has unique strengths.

For example, there is a strength that is given to man to protect and serve, and there is strength given to the woman for wisdom and nurturing. One is not the spiritual superior to the other, but they are a matching set—like King and Queen of hearts—designed to bless, strengthen, and complement each other.

You have so much more power and strength than you ever imagine. God had created the man first, then he said "It is not good for man to be alone, I will make a help meet for him." The woman is God's ideal, not man's. The word meet is the Hebrew word literally meaning to surround with. God in His infinite wisdom chose to surround his man with wisdom, knowledge, strength, assistance, and life—and all of this was wrapped up in, and embodied in the woman.

Chapter Nine

I want all my ladies to understand my heart on this. You can be strong and yet be tender at the same time. Look at Jesus.

I was a single parent after my husband divorced me. All I had or wanted was my two beautiful girls. God, who is the source of our strength, helped me to raise them. Now that's strength.

Let's go to the Word of God and find out about our strength.

Proverbs 31:10-31(KJV)

Who can find a virtuous woman? for her price is far above rubies. The heart of her husband doth safely trust in her, so that he shall have no need of spoil. She will do him good and not evil all the days of her life. She seeketh wool, and flax, and worketh willingly with her hands. She is like the merchants' ships; she bringeth her food from afar. She riseth also while it is yet night, and giveth meat to her household, and a portion to her maidens.

She considereth a field, and buyeth it: with the fruit of her hands she planteth a vineyard. **She girdeth**

her loins with strength, and strengtheneth her arms. *She perceiveth that her merchandise is good: her candle goeth not out by night. She layeth her hands to the spindle, and her hands hold the distaff. She stretcheth out her hand to the poor; yea, she reacheth forth her hands to the needy.*
She is not afraid of the snow for her household: for all her household are clothed with scarlet. She maketh herself coverings of tapestry; her clothing is silk and purple. Her husband is known in the gates, when he sitteth among the elders of the land. She maketh fine linen, and selleth it; and delivereth girdles unto the merchant.

Strength and honour are her clothing; and she shall rejoice in time to come. *She openeth her mouth with wisdom; and in her tongue is the law of kindness. She looketh well to the ways of her household, and eateth not the bread of idleness.*

Her children arise up, and call her blessed; her husband also, and he praiseth her. **Many daughters have done virtuously, but thou excellest them all.** *Favour is deceitful, and beauty is vain: but a woman that feareth the Lord, she shall be praised.*

Give her of the fruit of her hands; and let her own works praise her in the gates.

I want to emphasize the 17th and 25th verses because it talks about her strength. Verse 29 says there are many daughters but you excel them all, Glory to God.

You see, the secret of your strength is your connection to God, many times in the Book of Psalms it says the Lord is my strength. I came to understand this. The Lord is the source of my strength. The word *strength* signifies, *power, might, stronghold, fortification, strong-willed,* and even *stubborn.*

It is recorded that Samson the strongest man in the Bible—he had supernatural strength when God's Spirit would come upon him. He was so powerful that the Philistine armies trembled at the very mention of his name.

However, as strong as he was, he did not conquer Delilah. She conquered him. We cannot rely on our own strength, but the power that comes from His Spirit.

Zechariah 4:6 declares "Not by might, nor by power, but by my spirit, saith the Lord of hosts."

I believe the attributes of the Proverbs 31 woman are in every woman. Every woman has this potential for all these dimensions of strength dwelling on the inside of them. We just have to tap into all that God has given us by His Spirit, and receive all that God has promised.

Let's move on to compassion. Compassion is one of the most powerful words in the entire Bible. In its simplest term, it means to be tender-hearted.

> *Ezekiel 36:26 (KJV)*
> *A new heart also will I give you, and a new spirit will I put within you: and I will take away the stony heart out of your flesh, and I will give you an heart of flesh.*

In my life, I was tired of pain and betrayal. I once asked God to change my heart, so that I could never be hurt again. Of course, God told me "No."

What I was asking was completely opposite of what God wanted to do in me. His desire is always to take our hearts of stone and make them soft and tender hearts of flesh—hearts tender to Him so He can mold us, shape us, and write His Word on the tables of our heart.

My mentor once told me "Nindyl, you have to have T and T. You have to have a Tough hide and a Tender heart." Glory to God!

Throughout the book of Psalms, the Word tells us that God is full of compassion and full of grace.

> *Psalm 78:38 (KJV)*
> *But he, being full of compassion, forgave their iniquity, and destroyed them not: yea, many a time turned he his anger away, and did not stir up all his wrath.*

> *Psalm 86:15 (KJV)*
> *But thou, O Lord, art a God full of compassion, and gracious, longsuffering, and plenteous in mercy and truth.*

> *Psalm 111:4 (KJV)*
> *He hath made his wonderful works to be remembered: the Lord is gracious and full of compassion.*

> *Psalm 112:4 (KJV)*
> *Unto the upright there ariseth light in the darkness: he is gracious, and full of compassion, and righteous.*
>
> *Psalm 145:8 (KJV)*
> *The Lord is gracious, and full of compassion; slow to anger, and of great mercy.*

Of course I could give you more examples ... I really want you to get this in your spirit. God is not up in heaven anxiously waiting to judge you or send you to hell. He absolutely loves and adores you!

Our heavenly Father is full of grace and compassion ... period.

Compassion in the Hebrew language is the word *"Racham,"* which means to touch, to love, and especially denotes tender love, mercy, and kindness.

Now, let's look at Jesus. Is He like His Father in the area of compassion? Of course! I believe there was a great move of the Spirit throughout Jesus' ministry—I called it a move of compassion.

Matthew 15:32 (KJV)

Then Jesus called his disciples unto him, and said, I have compassion on the multitude, because they continue with me now three days, and have nothing to eat: and I will not send them away fasting, lest they faint in the way.

Matthew 15:32 (AMP)

Then Jesus called His disciples to Him, and said, "I feel compassion for the crowd, because they have been with Me now three days and have nothing [left] to eat; and I do not want to send them away hungry, because they might faint [from exhaustion] on the way [home]."

Mark 1:41 (KJV)

And Jesus, moved with compassion, put forth his hand, and touched him, and saith unto him, I will; be thou clean.

Mark 1:41 (AMP)

Moved with compassion [for his suffering], Jesus reached out with His hand and touched him, and said to him, "I am willing; be cleansed."

Luke 7:13 (KJV)

And when the Lord saw her, he had compassion on her, and said unto her, Weep not.

Luke 7:13 (AMP)

When the Lord saw her, He felt [great] compassion for her, and said to her, "Do not weep."

Luke 15:20 (KJV)

And he arose, and came to his father. But when he was yet a great way off, his father saw him, and had compassion, and ran, and fell on his neck, and kissed him.

Luke 15:20 (AMP)

So he got up and came to his father. But while he was still a long way off, his father saw him and was moved with compassion for him, and ran and embraced him and kissed him.

You see, Jesus was just like the Father—full of compassion—which moved him to action. But compassion is not like pity. Pity says "Oh I'm so sorry I wish I could help." Compassion is action. It has to move to heal, feed the hungry, and clothe the naked. Compassion must move.

We have to have the strength and courage to allow compassion to move us. Remember the Father is full of compassion, the son is full of compassion, and we are full of compassion.

Out Of the Compassion of God Comes His Tender Mercies

1 John 3:17 (AMP)
But whoever has the world's goods (adequate resources), and sees his brother in need, but has no compassion for him, how does the love of God live in him?

Colossians 3:12 (ASV)
Put on therefore, as God's elect, holy and beloved, a heart of compassion, kindness, lowliness, meekness, longsuffering; forbearing one another, and forgiving each other, if any man have a complaint against any; even as the Lord forgave you, so also do ye ...

Praise God! I am just like my Father, and just like my Savior! I am strong, full of might and power. I am strengthened by the Lord who is my source—He is the source of my strength, and He is the source and the reason for my heart of compassion. My God has given me a heart like His, and the power to conquer all my enemies.

Listen, Wonder Woman ain't got nothing on us! We are the mighty women of God, full of faith and power, full of might and wisdom, and full of God's grace and compassion. I am what He says I am, and I have what he says I can have, in Jesus' Name.

CHAPTER TEN

God's Love is Always First

Have you ever fallen so deeply in love, until you could not eat, sleep, or even think right? Well, I have. I mean I had it *bad!* I was so very much in love, so much so that this man literally became my world. I was so consumed with loving him. I only had eyes for him. He was a great desire … my dream come true.

And then I gave my heart to Jesus—it was at that instant that the man I loved seemed to change. However, no matter what he did or said, I still loved him deeply. When he would try to keep me from Jesus, I just loved Christ more and more.

In God, we need to understand our priorities for life. In the book of Genesis you can really find the answers every situation in life. So let's return to Genesis to find our true priorities.

You're Priorities for Life

#1. Your Personal Relationship to God Almighty

> *Genesis 2:5-9 (MSG)*
> *At the time God made Earth and Heaven, before any grasses or shrubs had sprouted from the*

ground—God hadn't yet sent rain on Earth, nor was there anyone around to work the ground (the whole Earth was watered by underground springs)—God formed Man out of dirt from the ground and blew into his nostrils the breath of life. The Man came alive—a living soul!

Then God planted a garden in Eden, in the east. He put the Man he had just made in it. God made all kinds of trees grow from the ground, trees beautiful to look at and good to eat. The Tree-of-Life was in the middle of the garden, also the Tree-of-Knowledge-of-Good-and-Evil.

When God created man, it was God and His man: so your first priority above all else is your personal relationship to Almighty God and this will ultimately affect everything else in your life.

#2. Your Wife or Husband That God Has Given You

Genesis 2:18 (AMP)
Now the Lord God said, "It is not good (beneficial) for the man to be alone; I will make him a helper [one who balances

him—a counterpart who is] suitable and complementary for him."

#3. Your Children

Genesis 1:28 (AMP)
And God blessed them [granting them certain authority] and said to them, "Be fruitful, multiply, and fill the earth, and subjugate it [putting it under your power]; and rule over (dominate) the fish of the sea, the birds of the air, and every living thing that moves upon the earth."

First: *God and Man*

Second: *God, Man, and Woman*

Third: *God, Man, Woman, and then Children (Be Fruitful)*

We must love God first, for He is the source of all love, he is also the initiator or our love relationship.

1 John 4:19 tells us, "We love Him because He first loved us."

This makes so much sense, because if my personal relationship with God is not right, I cannot treat Him with the spiritual love he truly deserves, and I cannot love my spouse correctly! If the husband and wife are not treating each other with the *agape* love that comes from God, the soil that the children are being grown in is not correct, and they will be brought up in an ungodly environment ... so begins a vicious cycle.

We must cultivate an environment of love in our personal relationship with God, and with our family.

#4. Your Job

Fourth: *The fourth priority is your job, ministry, etc.*

Although your job or ministry calling comes from God, always remember that the family came first— thousands of years before any other responsibility. "Family Ministry" (or ministering to your family) is before any other ministry. From a strong family foundation, healthy outreach ministry at your job or church can flow.

There is a story in the gospels that God that connected to my life because I see myself in this story so clearly. For the longest time, whenever I heard a preacher talk about this story, I would immediately be touched in my heart and begin to weep. I want to share this story with you to show the greatness of God and his love towards all mankind.

Matthew 9:18-22 (KJV)

While he spake these things unto them, behold, there came a certain ruler, and worshipped him, saying, My daughter is even now dead: but come and lay thy hand upon her, and she shall live. And Jesus arose, and followed him, and so did his disciples.

And, behold, a woman, which was diseased with an issue of blood twelve years, came behind him, and touched the hem of his garment: for she said within herself, If I may but touch his garment, I shall be whole.

But Jesus turned him about, and when he saw her, he said, Daughter, be of good comfort; thy faith hath made thee whole.

And the woman was made whole from that hour.

Chapter Ten

Matthew 9:18-22 (AMP)

While He was saying these things to them, a ruler (synagogue official) entered [the house] and kneeled down and worshiped Him, saying, "My daughter has just now died; but come and lay Your hand on her, and she will live." Jesus got up and began to accompany the ruler, with His disciples.

Then a woman who had suffered from a hemorrhage for twelve years came up behind Him and touched the [tassel] fringe of His outer robe; for she had been saying to herself, "If I only touch His outer robe, I will be healed." But Jesus turning and seeing her said, "Take courage, daughter; your [personal trust and confident] faith [in Me] has made you well." And at once the woman was [completely] healed.

I was very much like this woman, I was sick and had spent so much going to many doctors who could find nothing ... until one day a certain doctor found what was wrong with me. I, like this woman, decided to take it to the Lord. I decided to totally trust Him, to cast all my cares on Him. You know what? I went to church and Jesus completely healed me!

This woman had suffered greatly; she had this disease for twelve long years. It was like she had AIDS. She could not go to church because she was constantly bleeding. She could not come near, or touch anyone because of the blood. Even if she sat in a chair, they would burn the chair or the clothing she touched. It was really bad.

But then one day, she heard that this Jesus was going to be in town, and she decided right then and there she was going to reach Him. She said to herself, "If I can just touch the hem of his garment I know I will be made whole."

She heard the crowds, but she had to be very careful—she was not even supposed to be in the midst of this crowd. She could have been stomped or stoned to death, but she kept on going. She would not quit. She would not give up. She had been abused by many doctors until all her money was gone, but Doctor Jesus was in town! She crawled through the streets on a quiet mission, and finally, with all her might she reached up and touched the hem of his garment. She was made perfectly whole.

She received an instant miracle. She did not ask permission. She did not ask to have hands laid on her. She did not ask Jesus to come to her house and heal her. She believed by faith that Jesus was a miracle worker, and she took what she needed.

Isn't it amazing that Jesus was walking around the people every day full of healings, and full of miracles, waiting to be received by whoever asked? It is just like that today—His body is still carrying healings and miracles for all mankind. You just have to have faith to receive it for yourself!

Jesus was being grabbed and thronged by the multitude, but when this woman touched Him with a touch of faith, she immediately made an instant withdrawal from the bank of Jesus! Glory to God.

Jesus said, "someone touched me," and His disciples thought He was losing it because everybody was touching and grabbing Him. Jesus turned around and looked for her because he felt the power or virtue go out of His body because of her touch. Finally his eyes met her eyes, and she knew she was busted! She confessed, "It was me, Lord."

I praise God because Jesus said something that really makes the healing power of God available to all mankind. Jesus said "Thy Faith hast made thee whole." Wow! For those who would believe that healings and miracles are not for today, you also would have to say that faith is not for today either. If you say that, no one could get saved because we are saved by faith, and without faith, it's impossible to please God. The just live by faith, and without faith we would all be doomed.

Jesus did not fuss at her or tell her "How dare you to touch me!" Because of love and her faith, He blessed her life forever. Jesus' healings and miracles were ways to demonstrate the Father's love. They are God's divine calling card, designed to draw us into His love and into His kingdom.

A lot of people believe they are saved, but they haven't received Jesus as both Lord and Savior, placing

Him first above all else. You and I must be determined every single day to put Jesus first in all we say, think, and do.

God demonstrated His great love for us from the very beginning of time. When Adam sinned, God clothed Adam in a bloody sacrifice, which is a picture of us being covered by the Blood of Jesus. The entire Bible is a love story from beginning to end. God is constantly pursuing us to be his own, even to the point of sacrificing His only begotten Son, who shed His blood on Calvary's tree.

Romans 5:8 (AMP)
But God clearly shows and proves His own love for us, by the fact that while we were still sinners, Christ died for us.

Jesus was not just the High priest, He was also the sacrifice. He is the only High priest ever to take *His own blood* into the throne room of God. What love! Since He loved us first, and gave his life for you and me, the least we can do is give Him first place in our lives, and love God first.

I want to pray with you right now. If you don't know the love of Jesus, if you have not given your heart to Him, then today is your day! The Word of God says that when you hear His voice calling you, do not harden your heart. If you feel God is knocking on the door of your heart, open up and let Jesus in. My friend, He is knocking right now. Please give your heart to Jesus today. You've tried it your way. You have tried everything else—why not give my Jesus a chance.

Just say this out loud from your heart.

Jesus, I call on your name today. I need you in my heart and my life. Save me, Jesus, I surrender all. I have come to the end of myself, and I know I can't make it without you. Come into my heart today. Amen.

CHAPTER ELEVEN

Love Is Blind until God Opens Your Eyes

I used to always listen when people would say, "Love is blind. You don't understand it, and you have to. Just leave it." I use to wonder why I was so blind. But when you are deeply in love with someone, you begin to think that the person is the <u>most</u> beautiful person in the world—there is no other like that person.

I remember people used to tell me so many things about my ex-husband that was really hard for me to believe.

I always thought they're just jealous, but actually, I was blind. I was so in love that I was not able to see everything around me. I was more confused than anything else. My family used to say, "What is wrong with you? Open your eyes and see what you have in front of your face." I would get upset and say, "What are you talking about? I don't understand." The reality was I needed to love God and put Him first.

We need to be in love with Him more than anybody else. When you learn to do that then, God will put everything together for you.

Chapter Eleven

I went to the church one day, and it seemed like a cloud was covering my eyes. The pastor's wife prayed over me for me to see the light, and when she did my vision was brighter, the colors were beautiful and shining. Then I went home, and I started looking at everything from a different point of view. God opened my eyes, let me see what was really going on. I could see my life clearly and I made a decision. I prayed so hard and thanked God that He opened my eyes.

I saw so many different things—family, friends, ex-husband, coworkers—I had a brand new vision for all of them. When God did that, it felt so good! I felt like I was beautiful again! I was able to see myself in the mirror and say to myself, "You are beautiful and wonderful."

Many people used to tell me, "Nindyl, you're beautiful" but I never really believed them before. I never saw myself as a beautiful person. My dad used to tell me, "let people tell you that you're beautiful ... you don't tell people that." So when people would tell me that, it was hard for me to believe it.

Now that my eyes are open, I understand that I am blessed, I am beautiful and marvelous because Jesus made me. I am His creation fearfully and wonderfully made.

I was able to see myself. I was able to be proud of myself, and recognize everything that I had accomplished—everything that God helped me to get done. I had a decent job. I continue to fight like a lion. I can fly like an eagle. No matter what the enemy was trying, I was still fighting with the army of God on my side—the Father with the Holy Spirit, and fire with the Angels going first before me.

I was praising Him, dancing for God, and I never stop believing that He was going to do a miracle. He's done so many miracles and wonders for me! That's why I love Him. I am in love with Him. When you put God first, He will always be with you.

God opened my eyes, and now I can see everything. Amen.

Chapter Eleven

When you give your heart to God, He will literally change how you see things. The old folks used to sing a song that went like this: "I looked at my hands and they looked new, I looked at my feet and they did too."

Without Christ, you are blind, and having your understanding darkened; you cannot truly see how beautiful God is, and you surely can't see how beautiful you are.

Ephesians 1:18 (KJV)
... the eyes of your understanding being enlightened; that ye may know what is the hope of his calling, and what the riches of the glory of his inheritance in the saints ...

Ephesians 1:18 (AMP)
And [I pray] that the eyes of your heart [the very center and core of your being] may be enlightened [flooded with light by the Holy Spirit], so that you will know and cherish the hope [the divine guarantee, the confident expectation] to which He has called you, the riches of His glorious inheritance in the saints (God's people) ...

Ephesians 1:18 (NLT)

I pray that your hearts will be flooded with light so that you can understand the confident hope he has given to those he called—his holy people who are his rich and glorious inheritance.

Ephesians 4:18 (KJV)

… having the understanding darkened, being alienated from the life of God through the ignorance that is in them, because of the blindness of their heart …

Ephesians 4:18 (AMP)

… for their [moral] understanding is darkened and their reasoning is clouded; [they are] alienated and self-banished from the life of God [with no share in it; this is] because of the [willful] ignorance and spiritual blindness that is [deep-seated] within them, because of the hardness and insensitivity of their heart.

Chapter Eleven

> ***Ephesians 4:18 (NLT)***
> *Their minds are full of darkness; they wander far from the life God gives because they have closed their minds and hardened their hearts against him.*

There was a very mighty man in the Bible, who was known as the strong man in the Bible, but he was defeated by a woman because he was blinded by love.

Regarding Samson, I say he was blind twice. First he was blinded spiritually, which eventually led to him being blinded naturally.

> ***Judges 16:4-5, 20-21 (KJV)***
> *And it came to pass afterward, that he loved a woman in the valley of Sorek, whose name was Delilah. And the lords of the Philistines came up unto her, and said unto her, Entice him, and see wherein his great strength lieth, and by what means we may prevail against him, that we may bind him to afflict him: and we will give thee every one of us eleven hundred pieces of silver ...*

And she said, The Philistines be upon thee, Samson. And he awoke out of his sleep, and said, I will go out as at other times before, and shake myself. And he wist not that the Lord was departed from him.

But the Philistines took him, and put out his eyes, and brought him down to Gaza, and bound him with fetters of brass; and he did grind in the prison house.

Because of love and persistence by Delilah, Samson gave up the secret of his strength. In the past he would shake himself and the power of God would come on him. However, after he shared his secret, he shook and no strength came. He broke his covenant with God.

The Philistines took him, plucked his eyes out, and put him in prison. But aren't you glad God is the God of second chances?! Samson's hair began to grow back, Samson prayed to God, and his strength returned. It took Samson to lose his sight that he might again see God.

Please allow God to use your eyes. Learn to see life and this world through the eyes of God.

CHAPTER TWELVE

Tears of Blood

Have you ever asked God, "Why is this happening to me?"

When my husband left me I cried so much for three days. I couldn't sleep for 24 hours straight. I asked God to give my husband back. I cried and cried. I said, "Father all I did was go to church, trying to be a good woman. All I did was work hard and come straight home … why is this happening?"

Keep in mind that light and darkness tend to battle. As a married couple, if one person is called to ministry and one is not, there is going to be conflict.

I didn't understand the importance of God always being first. Many other people have made the same mistake; we are human.

The Holy Spirit used to wake me up at 3 o'clock in the morning, and I would use that time to pray and worship Him. I was praying and worshiping one night, and I asked God, "Why don't you dry my tears? I don't want to cry anymore. I am tired of crying like a baby for my husband to come back." It was so hard for me because I was so in love with Him. (He never believed me, but I guess I made him like my god).

That day at 3 o'clock in the morning was the time that I asked God to change my heart to the point that no one can hurt me anymore. I asked him three nights in a row, and I got the answer. "Daughter I can't change your heart. Your heart is the very reason I picked you; but I will mold it and you will be able to protect it in the future."

"Father, please dry my tears and make my heart like a rock ... I don't want to have feelings."

Every time I see somebody sad and in pain, it hurts my heart. I want to heal, protect, and help everyone. It was so hard for me to understand. He was not going to dry my tears and make my heart like a rock.

My eyes were so swollen and red. My daughter told me, "Mother, you need to sleep." I'd tell her, " I can't sleep." She would call me tell me everything's going to be OK. I would pretend to be strong, and then when she went into her room, I would cry again.

My daughter told me one day, "Mother, you are going to cry tears of blood one day. You are going to get sick crying so much." I told her, "I'm going to be ok. You're right—everything's gonna be fine. We are going to make it somehow. I don't know how, but we will, because my Father God will never leave us nor forsake us."

He was the only one I have, and the only one I need. He took all the tears and pain that I had to go through. I understand that without Him, I would've lost my mind.

I was going to the doctors telling them I couldn't sleep. One day, I made a decision. I said to myself, "God, send angels into my life so I can talk to them, and I can trust them with my testimony."

Then I started talking to the pastor's wife. I have so much respect for my pastors and honor them. They were there for me anytime I needed. I even called at 2 or 3 o'clock in the morning. They were available for me, anytime, day or night. I love them all. I respect my pastors. It was an honor to have them in my life.

Chapter Twelve

One day, God said to me, "What are they doing for you?"

You will be doing for other people, you will be counseling them and helping them, praying for them, and encouraging them. Now, I truly understand why I had to go through what I went through. A lot of people are ashamed to share their testimony. I'm not ashamed anymore. To me, my testimony is going to help others to speak the truth, and learn how to love one another. At the end of the day, love overcomes any situation.

Never forget, we have God's love with us and without Him we are nothing.

To finish this book I had drop tears of blood again because I had to bring back to my remembrance everything that I went through. I relived every moment, and I cried out while writing it. However, when everything is done, my tears will be tears of joy—unspeakable joy, happiness and love, peace and mercy. Jesus is worth it! I love him so much. God is my Father … my everything! He is my first and my last. Without Him I'm nothing.

Now for you that have cried tears of blood—crying through a pain so intense, you don't know how to describe it—I want you to know that Jesus knows exactly how you feel. He has experienced all suffering, agony, and pain, beyond anything you can imagine. He understands your pain, and He loves you more than you will ever know. Just call on Him, trust Him, and allow Him to heal you with His warm embrace.

CONCLUSION

By God's Design

As I look back through all the seasons of my life, I find myself in complete amazement. In every season—sorrows and joys, heartaches, and laughter of falling in love—one thing has become amazingly clear: God is the author of my story. He is the author and finisher of my life's script.

He has always been there. He said He would never leave me nor forsake me. He also said I will be with you always. God still has the pen in His hand, preparing to write the next chapters.

I am so excited to see where he is taking me! I am so hungry for my next level in God. I have come from having everything—being daddy's little princess living in Nicaragua to coming to the United States at the age of seventeen.

As I learn more about God and my Jesus, I learn everything is not always as it seems, and even in the worst times of my life, Jesus was with me every step of the way.

When Joseph was in the pit betrayed by his own brothers, he did not know he was going to be ruling in the palace. When he was enjoying life serving in Potiphar's house, he did not know he would soon spend many years in prison. But through it all, we see God's favor was on him, and his gifts from God never left him.

Many times, even when God gives you a vision or a dream, you see the end result of that dream or vision, but not all the details in regards to you accomplishing or fulfilling that dream.

God told the Children of Israel about the Promised Land, but that tiny thing He neglected to mention is that the land was filled with giant folks. You see, God did not mention it because it really was not relevant to them possessing the land. If God says the land is yours—I don't care who lives there—give them their eviction notice! Glory to God.

God has a perfect will, which we are quickly headed to. However, the most part, many of us are living in His permissive will. The world is not perfect, and we do have an enemy ... but God has always made a way out of no way. He has always given a way of escape.

2 Corinthians 2:14 tells us that our God always causes us to triumph! It did not say *sometimes*—it said *always*.

Isaiah 54:17 says "no weapon formed against you shall prosper."

David said in Psalm 37:25, "I have never seen the righteous forsaken or his seed begging bread."

God's love towards us is so incredibly amazing; He designed the world and the Universe just for us. Everything on this planet—the birds, the sky, and fish in the sea or the earth itself—testifies to the Glory of a magnificent loving Father.

Job 12:7-10 (KJV)

But ask now the beasts, and they shall teach thee; and the fowls of the air, and they shall tell thee: or speak to the earth, and it shall teach thee: and the fishes of the sea shall declare unto thee. Who knoweth not in all these that the hand of the Lord hath wrought this? In whose hand is the soul of every living thing, and the breath of all mankind.

Job 12:7-10 (AMP)

Now ask the animals, and let them teach you [that God does not deal with His creatures according to their character]; And ask the birds of the air, and let them tell you; Or speak to the earth [with its many forms of life], and it will teach you; And let the fish of the sea declare [this truth] to you.

Who among all these does not recognize **[in all these things that good and evil are randomly scattered throughout nature and human life]** *that the hand of the Lord has done this, in whose hand is the life of every living thing, And the breath of all mankind?*

Take a close look at the 9th verse; it says "who among these does not recognize, that good and evil are randomly scattered throughout nature and human life."

Wow! We see it in life. We see ups and downs in nature. We even see it in the weather pattern. But God is always right here with us!

As you look back through your life, never forget to see the beauty of God's Design.

I want you to know that you are in the midst of God's heart. You are the apple of His eye and He has great plans for you. You are His special treasure, and when you belong to Christ, your story is being written by God Himself.

Your path and your course is being personally directed by Him. Trust Him and know that your final outcome is By God's Design.

*** Deuteronomy 7:6 (AMP)***
For you are a holy people [set apart] to the Lord your God; the Lord your God has chosen you out of all the peoples on the face of the

earth to be a people for His own possession [that is, His very special treasure].

Jeremiah 29:11 (EXB)

I say this because I know ·what [L the plans] I am planning for you," says the LORD. "I have ·good plans for you [L plans for your peace/security], not plans ·to hurt you [L for your harm]. I will give you hope and a good future.

May God bless you and keep you, my precious friend. Thank you so much for honoring me by your purchase of my book.

I pray that it touches your life and the lives of many in Jesus' mighty name.

Nindyl Travers

www.ingramcontent.com/pod-product-compliance
Lightning Source LLC
Chambersburg PA
CBHW072053290426
44110CB00014B/1659